# Pigs and Dogs
## by Caryl Churchill

### Caryl Churchill (Writer)

Plays include: **Owners, Traps, Light Shining in Buckinghamshire, Cloud 9, Top Girls, Fen, Serious Money, Ice Cream, Mad Forest, The Skriker, Blue Heart, This is a Chair, Far Away, A Number, Drunk Enough To Say I Love You?, Seven Jewish Children, Love & Information, Here We Go, Escaped Alone.**

### Fisayo Akinade (Cast)

For the Royal Court: **The Crossings Plays.**

Other theatre includes: **The Tempest (Globe); Barbarians (Young Vic); The Vote (Donmar); As You Like It (New Wolsey); Refugee Boy, Waiting for Godot (West Yorkshire Playhouse); Neighbours (HighTide).**

Television includes: **In the Dark, A Midsummer Night's Dream, Ordinary Lies, Cucumber, Banana, Fresh Meat.**

Film includes: **The Girl with All the Gifts.**

### Sharon D Clarke (Cast)

Theatre includes: **Ma Rainey's Black Bottom, An Oak Tree, Everyman, 50 Years On Stage, Amen Corner (National); Romeo & Juliet (Rose, Kingston); Mother Goose, Puss In Boots, Blues in the Night, Vagina Monologues (Hackney Empire); Porgy & Bess (Regent's Park Open Air); Ghost, Hairspray, Chicago, We Will Rock You, The Lion King, Rent, Mama I Want To Sing (West End); Lift Off (Curve, Leicester); Once On This Island (Birmingham Rep/Peacock/Nottingham Playhouse/Hackney Empire); Little Shop of Horrors (Haymarket, Leicester).**

Television includes: **You Me & Them, Death in Paradise, New Tricks, Psychobitches, Justin's House, Tree Fu Tom, EastEnders, The Shadow Line, The Bill, Holby City, Last Choir Standing, Waking the Dead.**

Film includes: **Sugarhouse, Secret Society, Beautiful People, Broken Glass, Tumble Down.**

Awards include: **Olivier Award for Best Supporting Actress (Amen Corner); Manchester Theatre Award for Best Actress (Ghost); TV Screen Nation Award for Best Actress (Holby City); What's On Stage Theatregoers Choice Award for Best Supporting Actress (We Will Rock You).**

### Dominic Cooke (Director)

For the Royal Court: **The Low Road, In Basildon, Ding Dong the Wicked, In the Republic of Happiness, Choir Boy, Clybourne Park (& West End), Chicken Soup with Barley, Aunt Dan & Lemon, The Fever, Seven Jewish Children, Wig Out!, Now or Later, Fear & Misery/War & Peace, Rhinoceros, The Pain & The Itch, Other People, Fireface, Spinning Into Butter, Redundant, F***ing Games, Plasticine, The People Are Friendly, This is a Chair, Identical Twins.**

Other theatre includes: **Ma Rainey's Black Bottom, Here We Go, The Comedy of Errors (National); Teddy Ferrara (Donmar); Arabian Nights (Young Vic/UK & World Tour/Off Broadway); Noughts & Crosses, Pericles, The Winter's Tale, The Crucible, Postcards from America, As You Like It, Macbeth, Cymbeline, The Malcontent (RSC); By the Bog of Cats (West End); The Eccentricities of a Nightingale (Gate, Dublin); The Weavers, Hunting Scenes from Lower Bavaria (Gate); The Bullet (Donmar); Afore Night Come, Entertaining Mr Sloane (Clwyd); The Importance of Being Earnest (Atlantic Theatre Festival, Canada); My Mother Said I Never Should (Oxford Stage Company/Young Vic); Kiss of the Spider Woman (Bolton Octagon); Of Mice & Men (Nottingham Playhouse); Autogeddon (Assembly Rooms).**

Opera includes: **The Magic Flute (WNO); I Capuleti E I Montecchi, La bohème (Grange Park Opera).**

Television includes: **The Hollow Crown: The Wars of the Roses**

Awards include: **Olivier Awards for Best Director (The Crucible) & Best Revival (Ma Rainey's Black Bottom); International Theatre Institute Award for Excellence in International Theatre; TMA Award for Best Show for Children & Young People (Arabian Nights); Fringe First Award (Autogeddon).**

Dominic was the Artistic Director of the Royal Court from 2007 – 2013. In 2014 he was awarded a CBE for his services to Drama.

### Alex Hassell (Cast)

Theatre includes: **Henry IV Parts 1&2, Henry V (RSC/Barbican/BAM); Death of a Salesman (West End); A Midsummer Night's Dream, The City Madam, Cardenio, Othello (RSC); The Caretaker (Liverpool Everyman/Theatre Royal, Bath/BAM); Turandot (Hampstead); The Seagull, Hamlet (The Factory); I Am Shakespeare (Chichester Festival); The Tempest, The Storm, Measure for Measure (Globe); A Midsummer's Night Dream**

(Orchestra of the Age of Enlightenment); Blood & Ice (Royal Lyceum, Edinburgh); Hardcore (Pleasance, Edinburgh).

Television includes: **Silent Witness, Way to Go, Big Thunder, Life of Crime, Hustle, A Cop in Paris, Miranda, Love Soup, Bonkers, Torchwood, Queen of Swords, Robin Hood, Murphy's Law, Pepys, Boudicca, Death in Holy Orders, Danielle Cable: Eyewitness, Murder In Mind, Kenneth Tynan: In Praise of Hardcore, Hawkins.**
**Film includes: Miss in Her Teens, Anonymous, Two Down, The Sick House, Cold Mountain, Calendar Girls.**

Radio includes: **The Changeling.**

**Alex is the Artistic Director of The Factory.**

## David McSeveney (Sound Designer)

For the Royal Court: **Cyprus Avenue (& Abbey, Dublin), Lela & Co., Constellations (& West End/Broadway/Tour), Teh Internet Is Serious Business, The Art of Dying, Not 1/Footfalls/ Rockaby (& West End/National Tour/ International Tour), The Djinns of Eidgah, Routes, If You Don't Let Us Dream We Won't Let You Sleep, Belong, Vera Vera Vera, The Village Bike, Clybourne Park (& West End), Ingredient X, Posh (& West End), Disconnect, Cock, A Miracle, The Stone, Shades, Seven Jewish Children, The Girlfriend Experience (& Theatre Royal Plymouth/Young Vic), Contractions, Fear & Misery/War & Peace.**

Other theatre includes: **The Skriker (Royal Exchange/MIF); Blurred Lines (National); Macbeth, The Changeling (Young Vic); A Doll's House (Young Vic/West End/Brooklyn Academy of Music, New York); Wolf in Snakeskin Shoes, Stones in his Pockets (Tricycle); The Duke in Darkness (Tabard); The Winter's Tale (RSC); Victoria Station/One for the Road (Print Room/ Young Vic); On The Record (Arcola); The Tin Horizon (503); Gaslight (Old Vic); Charley's Aunt, An Hour & a Half Late (Theatre Royal, Bath); A Passage to India, After Mrs Rochester, Madame Bovary (Shared Experience); Men Should Weep, Rookery Nook (Oxford Stage Company); Othello (Southwark Playhouse).**

**David is Head of Sound at the Royal Court.**

## Jack Williams (Lighting Designer)

As Lighting Designer, for the Royal Court: **Ding Dong The Wicked, If You Don't Let Us Dream We Won't Let You Sleep, The Art of Dying, Peckham: The Soap Opera.**

As Associate Designer, for the Royal Court: **Beckett Trilogy (& National Tour/International Tour).**

As Lighting Designer, other theatre includes: **Mydidae (Soho/Trafalgar Studios); The Armour (Defibrillator).**

As Associate Designer, other theatre includes: **Ragtime, Midsummer Night's Dream (Regents Park Open Air); Dr. Strangelove (Secret Cinema).**
As Assistant Designer, other theatre includes: **The Magic Flute, Albert Herring (British Youth Opera).**

**Jack is Head of Lighting at the Royal Court.**

# THE ROYAL COURT THEATRE

**The Royal Court Theatre is the writers' theatre. It is the leading force in world theatre for energetically cultivating writers – undiscovered, emerging and established.**

**Through the writers, the Royal Court is at the forefront of creating restless, alert, provocative theatre about now. We open our doors to the unheard voices and free thinkers that, through their writing, change our way of seeing.**

Over 120,000 people visit the Royal Court in Sloane Square, London, each year and many thousands more see our work elsewhere through transfers to the West End and New York, UK and international tours, digital platforms, our residencies across London, and our site-specific work. Through all our work we strive to inspire audiences and influence future writers with radical thinking and provocative discussion.

The Royal Court's extensive development activity encompasses a diverse range of writers and artists and includes an ongoing programme of writers' attachments, readings, workshops and playwriting groups. Twenty years of the International Department's pioneering work around the world means the Royal Court has relationships with writers on every continent.

Within the past sixty years, John Osborne, Samuel Beckett, Arnold Wesker, Ann Jellicoe, Howard Brenton and David Hare have started their careers at the Court.

Many others including Caryl Churchill, Athol Fugard, Mark Ravenhill, Simon Stephens, debbie tucker green, Sarah Kane; and, more recently, Lucy Kirkwood, Nick Payne, Penelope Skinner and Alistair McDowall, have followed.

The Royal Court has produced many iconic plays from Laura Wade's **Posh** to Jez Butterworth's **Jerusalem** and Martin McDonagh's **Hangmen**.

Royal Court plays from every decade are now performed on stage and taught in classrooms and universities across the globe.

**It is because of this commitment to the writer that we believe there is no more important theatre in the world than the Royal Court.**

Supported using public funding by
**ARTS COUNCIL ENGLAND**

# ROYAL

## COMING UP AT THE ROYAL COURT

### JERWOOD THEATRE DOWNSTAIRS

Until 6 Aug
**Unreachable**
written and directed by Anthony Neilson

15 Sep - 22 Oct
**Father Comes Home From The Wars
(Parts 1, 2 & 3)**
by Suzan-Lori Parks

17 Nov - 14 Jan
**The Children**
by Lucy Kirkwood

25 Jan - 11 Feb
**Escaped Alone**
by Caryl Churchill

### JERWOOD THEATRE UPSTAIRS

7 Sep - 15 Oct
**Torn**
by Nathaniel Martello-White

20 - 29 Oct
The Royal Court Theatre, house, and HighTide
present The HighTide Production
**Harrogate**
by Al Smith

10 Nov - 22 Dec
**The Sewing Group**
by E V Crowe

10 Jan - 11 Feb
Royal Court Theatre and Royal Exchange Theatre
**WISH LIST**
by Katherine Soper

# royalcourttheatre.com

JERWOOD **CHARITABLE** FOUNDATION

Torn is part of the Royal Court's Jerwood New Playwrights
programme, supported by the Jerwood Charitable Foundation.

Supported using public funding by
**ARTS COUNCIL
ENGLAND**

Sloane Square London, SW1W 8AS
🐦 royalcourt 👍 royalcourttheatre
🚇 Sloane Square 🚉 Victoria Station

# COURT

# ROYAL COURT SUPPORTERS

The Royal Court is a registered charity and not-for-profit company. We need to raise £1.7 million every year in addition to our core grant from the Arts Council and our ticket income to achieve what we do.

We have significant and longstanding relationships with many generous organisations and individuals who provide vital support. Royal Court supporters enable us to remain the writers' theatre, find stories from everywhere and create theatre for everyone.

We can't do it without you.

Coutts supports innovation at the Royal Court. The Genesis Foundation supports the Royal Court's work with International Playwrights. Bloomberg supports Beyond the Court. Jerwood Charitable Foundation supports emerging writers through the Jerwood New Playwrights series. The Pinter Commission is given annually by his widow, Lady Antonia Fraser, to support a new commission at the Royal Court.

## PUBLIC FUNDING

Arts Council England, London
British Council

## CHARITABLE DONATIONS

The Austin & Hope
Pilkington Trust
Martin Bowley Charitable Trust
The City Bridge Trust
The Clifford Chance
Foundation
Cockayne - Grants for the Arts
The Ernest Cook Trust
Cowley Charitable Trust
The Dorset Foundation
The Eranda Foundation
Lady Antonia Fraser for
The Pinter Commission
Genesis Foundation
The Golden Bottle Trust

The Haberdashers' Company
Roderick & Elizabeth Jack
Jerwood Charitable
Foundation
Kirsh Foundation
The Mackintosh Foundation
Marina Kleinwort Trust
The Andrew Lloyd Webber
Foundation
The London Community
Foundation
John Lyon's Charity
Clare McIntyre's Bursary
The Andrew W. Mellon
Foundation
The Mercers' Company
The Portrack Charitable Trust
The David & Elaine Potter
Foundation
The Richard Radcliffe
Charitable Trust
Rose Foundation
Royal Victoria Hall Foundation
The Sackler Trust
The Sobell Foundation
John Thaw Foundation
The Vandervell Foundation
Sir Siegmund Warburg's
Voluntary Settlement
The Garfield Weston
Foundation
The Wolfson Foundation

## CORPORATE SPONSORS

AKA
AlixPartners
Aqua Financial Solutions Ltd
Bloomberg
Colbert
Coutts
Edwardian Hotels, London
Fever-Tree
Gedye & Sons

Kudos
MAC
Nyetimber

## BUSINESS MEMBERS

Auerbach & Steele
Opticians
CNC – Communications &
Network Consulting
Cream
Hugo Boss UK
Lansons
Left Bank Pictures
Rockspring Property
Investment Managers
Tetragon Financial Group
Vanity Fair

## DEVELOPMENT COUNCIL

Majella Altschuler
Piers Butler
Sarah Chappatte
Cas Donald
Celeste Fenichel
Piers Gibson
Emma Marsh
Angelie Moledina
Anatol Orient
Andrew Rodger
Deborah Shaw
Sian Westerman

Innovation partner

Supported using public funding by
**ARTS COUNCIL ENGLAND**

**Royal Court Theatre**
Sloane Square,
London SW1W 8AS
Tel: 020 7565 5050
info@royalcourttheatre.com
www.royalcourttheatre.com

Artistic Director
**Vicky Featherstone**
Executive Producer
**Lucy Davies**

Associate Directors
**Lucy Morrison, Hamish Pirie, John Tiffany, Graham Whybrow**
Associate Designer
**Chloe Lamford**
Associate Playwright
**Simon Stephens**
Associate Artists
**Carrie Cracknell, Katie Mitchell**

Artistic Associate
**Ola Animashawun**
Trainee Director
**Grace Gummer‡**

International Director
**Elyse Dodgson**
Associate Director
(International)
**Sam Pritchard**
International Assistant
**Sarah Murray**

General Manager
**Catherine Thornborrow**
Assistant Producer
**Minna Sharpe**
Projects Producer
**Chris James**
Assistant to the Executive
**Ryan Govin**
Trainee Administrator
(Producing)
**Jerome Mitchell§**
Trainee Administrator
(Projects & Literary)
**Zahra Beswick§**
Community Producer
(Tottenham & Pimlico)
**Chris Sonnex***

Deputy Head of Young Court
**Romana Flello**
Young Court Assistant
**Maia Clarke**

Literary Manager
**Christopher Campbell**
Deputy Literary Manager
**Louise Stephens**
Literary Assistant
**Adam Narat**

Head of Casting
**Amy Ball**
Casting Assistant
**Arthur Carrington**

Head of Production
**Matt Noddings**
Production Manager
**Marius Rønning**
Head of Lighting
**Jack Williams**
Lighting Deputy
**Steven Binks**
Lighting Technicians
**Jess Faulks, Matthew Harding**
JTD Programmer & Operator
**Catriona Carter**
Head of Stage
**Steven Stickler**
Stage Deputy
**Dan Lockett**
Stage Chargehand
**Lee Crimmen**
Chargehand & Building Maintenance Technician
**Matt Livesey**
Head of Sound
**David McSeveney**
Sound Deputy
**Emily Legg**
Head of Costume
**Lucy Walshaw**
Wardrobe Manager
**Gina Lee**
Costume Apprentice
**Courtney Musselwhite**
Company Manager
**Joni Carter**

Finance Director
**Helen Perryer**
Financial Controller
**Ed Hales**
Financial Administrator
**Rosie Mortimer**
Accounts Assistant
**Sian Ruffles**
Finance Trainee
**Kadisha Williams§**

Head of Press & Publicity
**Anoushka Hay**
Communications Trainee
(Press)
**Daniela Lewy§**

Head of Marketing
**Holly Conneely**
Marketing Manager
**Dion Wilson**
Marketing Officer
**Alex Green**
Communications Trainee
(Marketing)
**Audrey Aidoo-Davies§**

Head of Sales
**Liam Geoghegan**
Box Office Manager
**Helen Corbett**
Box Office Sales Assistants
**Will Bourdillon***,
**Laura Duncanson, Joe**

Hodgson, Margaret Perry***

Development Director
**Rebecca Kendall**
Deputy Development Director (Maternity Leave)
**Lucy Buxton**
Deputy Development Director (Maternity Cover)
**Liv Nilssen**
Senior Individual Giving Manager (Maternity Leave)
**Sue Livermore***
Development Manager
**Luciana Lawlor**
Corporate & Events Manager
**Nadia Vistisen**

Theatre Manager
**Rachel Dudley**
Senior Duty House Manager
**Adam Lawler**
Duty House Managers
**Flo Bourne, Elinor Keber, Tanya Shields**
Caretaker
**Christian Rudolph**
Bar & Kitchen Manager
**Ali Christian**
Deputy Bar & Kitchen Manager
**Robert Smael**
Assistant Bar & Kitchen Manager
**Jared Thomas**
Head Chef
**Francesco Ripanti**
Bookshop Manager
**Simon David**
Bookshop Assistant
**Eleanor Crosswell***

Stage Door/Reception
**Paul Lovegrove, Tiiu Mortley, Jane Wainwright**

Thanks to all of our Ushers and Bar & Kitchen staff.

§
Posts supported by
The Sackler Trust
Trainee Scheme

‡
The post of Trainee Director
is supported
by an anonymous donor.

* Part-time.
**ENGLISH STAGE COMPANY**

President
**Dame Joan Plowright CBE**

Honorary Council
**Sir Richard Eyre CBE**

**Alan Grieve CBE**
**Phyllida Lloyd CBE**
**Martin Paisner CBE**

Council Chairman
**Anthony Burton CBE**
Vice Chairman
**Graham Devlin CBE**
Members
**Jennette Arnold OBE**
**Judy Daish**
**Sir David Green KCMG**
**Joyce Hytner OBE**
**Stephen Jeffreys**
**Emma Marsh**
**Roger Michell**
**James Midgley**
**Anita Scott**
**Lord Stewart Wood**

# Remember the Royal Court in your will and help to ensure that our future is as iconic as our past.

Every gift, whatever the amount, will help us maintain and care for the building, support the next generation of playwrights starting out in their career, deliver our education programme and put our plays on the stage.

**LEAVE A LEGACY**

**To discuss leaving a legacy to the Royal Court, please contact:**

Sue Livermore, Senior Individual Giving Manager,
Royal Court Theatre, Sloane Square,
London, SW1W 8AS

**Email:** suelivermore@royalcourttheatre.com
**Tel:** 020 7565 5079

# PIGS AND DOGS

## Caryl Churchill

Three actors, any gender or race but not all the same. Each can play any character, regardless of the character's race or gender.

A dash – means a new speaker.

The play is substantially based on material from *Boy-Wives and Female Husbands* by Stephen O. Murray and Will Roscoe.

*This text went to press before the end of rehearsals and so may differ slightly from the play as performed.*

— Somebody says

— President of Gambia

— We will fight these vermins
the way we fight malaria-bearing mosquitoes.

— Somebody says

— President Mugabe

— If dogs and pigs don't do it
why must human beings?

— Somebody posts

— You western-backed goats.
They forced us into slavery and killed millions.
Now they want to downplay the sinfulness of
    homos.
It shall not work.

— Somebody says

— Zuma, South Africa

— When I was growing up an ungqingili
would not have stood before me.
I would knock him out.


— Uganda.
Anti Homosexuality Act 2014.

Death penalty.
Later amended
to life imprisonment.


—     I know I shouldn't have sent him to that white
        school.


—     Somebody says

—     Ethics Minister in Uganda

—     If I kissed a man
        I think I should die, I could not exist.
        It is inhuman.
        Just imagine
        Eating your own faeces.

—     Newspaper says

—     Two hundred top homosexuals.

—     Names, pictures.

—     Hang them.


—     Museveni says

—     President of Uganda

—     Ugandan independence in the face of western
        pressure.

—     Mugabe says

—   President of Zimbabwe

—   We have our own culture.


—   Somebody says

—   in America

—   member of a rap group

—   There is no word in any African language that
    describes homosexual.

—   But

—   sagoda never marry and wear skirts

—   ashtime dress like women and do women's work

—   mumenke is a man-woman

—   wasagu is a lesbian

—   yau dauda

—   unekonotsi

—   bifi

—   togo

—   kitesha

—   chibadi

—   omazenge

—   wobo.

—   If I had been a man
    I could have taken a wife and begat children.

If I had been a woman
I could have taken a husband and borne children.
But I am neither. I am wobo.


—     Somebody says

—     in America

—     intellectual

—     Homosexuality
       is not always a conceptual category.

—     Hausa, yau dauda

—     Yes, I'm yau dauda, we dress like women,
       we sing and dance and serve the fried chicken.
       We can still get married and give a girl children.
       You don't have to love her to give a girl children.


—     Hausa

—     Kwazo means work and that's male.
       Haja means goods and that's female.

—     Two men can be kwazo and haja.

—     An old woman can be kwazo and her young
               husband is the haja
       because she has the power.

—     Two women together is kifi
       when the two have equal power.
       Two men together can be kifi
       if they both have equal power.

—     It's play, wasa, play.

— You want someone and it's iskanci,

— craziness.


— Somebody says

— Evans-Pritchard, anthropologist, last century

— My informant Kuabia says

— this is how it used to be with the Zande.

— The boy's my wife.
I asked for his hand with five spears
the same way you ask for a maiden.
That man who had sex with him must pay me
    compensation.
Soon he'll choose his own boy-wife like all the
    warriors,
I'll find another one.
When a prince dies his boys are killed so no one
    else can have them.


— A king of the Maale in Ethiopia

— a long time ago

— the king could say

— Because I'm king I'm the most male man.
Everyone below me is less and less,
and least male of all is the ashtime.
The night before a ritual I must abstain from
    women.
I'm happy with my ashtime.

–     Nzinga of Ndongo

–     seventeenth century

–     succeeded her brother.

–     I am the king, I dress as a man.
      I have a harem of men dressed as women.
      I raised an army to fight the Portuguese
      and kept Ndongo free for forty years.


–     Musaji the first
      queen of the Lovedu

–     this is Lesotho, nineteenth century

–     I have a harem
      they are all young women.
      I am helped to rule
      by mothers of the kingdom.
      There are many queens
      among Bantu people.


–     Women in Dahomey

–     eighteenth century

–     soldiers.

–     We never get married, we live like men.
      Prostitutes are kept for us like for the men.

–     We marched against the Attahpahms as if they
           were men
      but we found them women
      and defeated them.

—    We are no longer women.
       We are men.


—    The Fou in Dahomey

—    When we stop being small
       we're kept from the girls
       so we turn to each other.

—    Most of us grow up to take women for wives.

—    But we've stayed together
       all our lives.


—    And a woman in Ghana

—    This is not so long ago

—    We girls had each other,
       now we're married.
       We buy big beds
       and still meet each other.


—    Again in Ghana

—    Man or woman,
       if you have a heavy soul
       you desire a woman.
       Man or woman,
       if you have a light soul
       you desire a man.

–    Somebody says

–    Nuer in Ethiopia

–    Men here don't have sex with men.
It's different with that man because he's a woman.
It was decided by a prophet of Denge
and now she can take a husband like a woman.


–    In Lesotho
a woman says

–    I chose this woman as my friend.
We have two feasts with both our husbands,
killing sheep and dancing and singing,
gifts and guests, just like a wedding.

–    A woman of ninetyseven says

–    Haven't you ever fallen in love with another girl?

–    In Lesotho
a woman says

–    In Lesotho
women like to kiss each other.
And it's nothing. Except sometimes.


–    Somebody says in Burkina Faso

–    Gender is not the same as anatomy.
The earth is very delicate machinery
with high vibration points,
and some people must be the guardians
to keep the continuity
with the spirits of this world and the other.

The one who binds the spirits is the gatekeeper.
His vibrational consciousness is far higher
and that makes him gay.
You don't get chosen,
you choose it yourself before you're born.
You come into the world with that vibration
and the Elders know you're connected to
    a gateway.


\—    English law.

\—    English law says 1533

\—    Forasmuch as there is not yet sufficient
and condign punishment
for the detestable and abominable
vice of buggery,
it may please the King's Highness
with the assent of the Lords Spiritual
and the Commons of this present Parliament
that the same offence be henceforth judged
    a felony.

\—    Hang them.


\—    Somebody says

\—    Englishman in Angola
sixteenth century

\—    They are beastly in their living
for they have men in women's apparel
whom they keep among their wives.

–    A missionary says

–    Seventeenth century

–    Sodomy is rampant in the south of Angola.

–    Missionaries, missionaries

–    Unnatural damnation

–    Detestable vices

–    Forsaking the natural use of women

–    Copulation contre nature.


–    Seventeenth century

–    Father Cavazzi

–    in the Congo as a missionary.

–    The Ganga-ya-Chibanda
is the most powerful Ganga.
He dresses like a woman
and is called the Grandmother.
He dresses
for sacrifices
in the skin
of a lion.
He has bells to call the gods of peace
and spirits of the dead.
He kills a snake,
a dog or a cock,
they bury the dog's head.
And the spirits show him where to find it.
Of course it's a trick,
he's told where to find it.

When he dies
he's buried at night
with such indecent ceremonies
the page would blush, so I can't write it.
They pull out his heart and liver
and hack off his toes and fingers
and sell them as relics.
And the colonial governor
can do nothing at all without the help of
    the Ganga.

—    Father Cavazzi says

—    This information is for the missionaries
consecrated to the people's instruction.
Somewhat fruitless up to now.


—    Somebody says

—    Italian explorer 1900

—    Men in Eritrea
sleep with little devils.
No one thinks it's evil.
Diavoletti.

—    Somebody says

—    German anthropologist 1923

—    Homosexual intercourse
from Orange to the Congo.
It's generally widespread.

—     The laws against sodomy
      were imported to the colonies.
      Repealed in Britain
      but thriving in the colonies.
      Thriving in the countries
      that used to be colonies.

—     We try them in the courts.

—     They had connection

—     fundamental orifice

—     obtained his purpose.

—     I was only playing.


—     Beating your wife

—     (She ends up dead)

—     Three months in prison.

—     Emitting semen on another man's legs

—     Six months in prison.


—     Somebody says

—     Ovambo chief

—     I know it is forbidden.
      I shoot them with my Browning.

–    Museveni says

–    President of Uganda

–    2014

–    This Act that we have passed
shows our independence
independence in the face of western pressure.


–    We have our own culture.

–    We will fight these vermins.

–    They are beasts of the forest

–    Mad people and criminals

–    Hand them over to the police

–    You cannot have a right to be a sick human being

–    Homosexuality will destroy humanity because
there's no procreation

–    There is no right in homosexuality

–    It is sub-animal behaviour, we will not allow it

–    If they don't like it they can leave

–    It is unAfrican

–    It is inconsistent with African values and belief in
the clan

–    It is unnatural behaviour and strange to our
culture.

–    Somebody says

–     Winnie Mandela

–     It is alien to our culture. It is filth.


–     Somebody says

–     American evangelists

–     We're losing America.

–     We're winning in Africa.


–     American evangelist

–     Gays are the agents
of America's moral decline.
The force behind Nazi atrocities.
If they could get away with killing
anyone opposed to them like yours truly,
they'd do it.
They have the media, academia, Hollywood,
    big corporations,
mental health associations,
even the US military.
Uganda can be a country led by God.

–     American evangelist goes to Kampala, says

–     Homosexuals have a hidden and dark agenda.
Evil.
They threaten the marriage based society.

— Ugandan legislator says
 at a Family Breakfast

— (this is a secret Christian organisation,
 American organisation)

— Let's consider execution.


— American evangelist says

— We're not involved in US politics
 much less in the politics of another nation.
 I don't support the death penalty
 but I support the Bill.
 I support the stand against evil.
 Winning in Africa.



— We have our own culture.



— Somebody says, somebody says

— Either is equally good and beautiful.

— I didn't know it was a crime.

— If I wanted to have a woman I can get plenty.

— Yes, we know that, we all do it.

— I never noticed anything peculiar, he worked as
  a nurse, I thought him sound in his mind.

— Why should we worry since we can't get pregnant?

–     Just staying together nicely.

–     People now don't love like they did long ago.

–     I was welcomed by his family.

–     We loved them better.


–     Somebody says

–     a Khoikhoi man

–     I wanted him so I gave him a cup of Sore-water.
      Nice when it's coffee but water will do.
      I said Sore-gansa-we!
      Drink the Sore-water!
      And he took it in his hands and drank it
      which means Yes.


–     It's wasa, play.

–     It's iskanci, craziness.

–     Sometimes for all our lives.

**Other works by Caryl Churchill, published by Nick Hern Books**

*Light Shining in Buckinghamshire*
*Traps*
*Cloud Nine*
*Icecream*
*Mad Forest*
*The Skriker*
*Thyestes* (translated from Seneca)
*Hotel*
*This is a Chair*
*Blue Heart*
*Far Away*
*A Number*
*A Dream Play* (translated from Strindberg)
*Drunk Enough to Say I Love You?*
*Bliss* (translated from Olivier Choinière)
*Seven Jewish Children – a play for Gaza*
*Love and Information*
*Ding Dong the Wicked*
*Here We Go*
*Escaped Alone*

**Collections**

*Plays: Three*
    *A Mouthful of Birds* (with David Lan)
    *Icecream*
    *Mad Forest*
    *Lives of the Great Poisoners* (with Orlando Gough and Ian Spink)
    *The Skriker*
    *Thyestes*

*Plays: Four*
    *Hotel*
    *This is a Chair*
    *Blue Heart*
    *Far Away*
    *A Number*
    *A Dream Play* (translated from Strindberg)
    *Drunk Enough to Say I Love You?*

*Shorts*
    *Lovesick*
    *Abortive*
    *Not Not Not Not Not Enough Oxygen*
    *Schreber's Nervous Illness*
    *The Hospital at the Time of the Revolution*
    *The Judge's Wife*
    *The After-Dinner Joke*
    *Seagulls*
    *Three More Sleepless Nights*

Rona Munro
THE ASTRONAUT'S CHAIR
THE HOUSE OF BERNARDA ALBA *after* Lorca
THE INDIAN BOY
IRON
THE JAMES PLAYS
THE LAST WITCH
LITTLE EAGLES
LONG TIME DEAD
THE MAIDEN STONE
MARY BARTON *after* Gaskell
PANDAS
SCUTTLERS
STRAWBERRIES IN JANUARY *from* de la Chenelière
YOUR TURN TO CLEAN THE STAIR & FUGUE

Paul Murphy
VALHALLA

James Rushbrooke
TOMCAT

Stef Smith
HUMAN ANIMALS
REMOTE
SWALLOW

Jack Thorne
2ND MAY 1997
BUNNY
BURYING YOUR BROTHER IN THE PAVEMENT
HOPE
JACK THORNE PLAYS: ONE
LET THE RIGHT ONE IN *after* John Ajvide Lindqvist
MYDIDAE
THE SOLID LIFE OF SUGAR WATER
STACY & FANNY AND FAGGOT
WHEN YOU CURE ME

Enda Walsh
ARLINGTON
BALLYTURK
BEDBOUND & MISTERMAN
DELIRIUM
DISCO PIGS & SUCKING DUBLIN
ENDA WALSH PLAYS: ONE
ENDA WALSH PLAYS: TWO
MISTERMAN
THE NEW ELECTRIC BALLROOM
ONCE
PENELOPE
ROALD DAHL'S THE TWITS
THE SMALL THINGS
THE WALWORTH FARCE

Alexandra Wood
THE ELEVENTH CAPITAL
THE EMPTY QUARTER
THE HUMAN EAR
THE INITIATE
MERIT
UNBROKEN

**A Nick Hern Book**

*Pigs and Dogs* first published in Great Britain as a paperback original in 2016 by Nick Hern Books Limited, The Glasshouse, 49a Goldhawk Road, London W12 8QP, in association with the Royal Court Theatre, London

*Pigs and Dogs* copyright © 2016 Caryl Churchill Limited

Caryl Churchill has asserted her right to be identified as the author of this work

Cover image: Dion Wilson

Designed and typeset by Nick Hern Books
Printed in Great Britain by Mimeo Ltd, Huntingdon, Cambridgeshire PE29 6XX

A CIP catalogue record for this book is available from the British Library

ISBN    978 1 84842 609 2

**Woodland**
**CARBON**
www.woodlandcarbon.co.uk
NICK HERN BOOKS
Printed on Carbon Captured paper

**www.nickhernbooks.co.uk**

facebook.com/nickhernbooks

twitter.com/nickhernbooks